Behind the Glamour

BEHIND [THE] SCENES
MOVIE CAREERS

By Danielle S. Hammelef

CAPSTONE PRESS
a capstone imprint

Savvy Books are published by Capstone Press,
1710 Roe Crest Drive, North Mankato, Minnesota 56003
www.mycapstone.com

Library of Congress cataloging-in-publication data is available on the Library of Congress website.

ISBN: 978-1-5157-4899-1 (hardcover) -- 978-1-5157-4912-7 (eBook PDF)

Summary: A behind-the-scenes look at some of the most interesting jobs that take place behind the glamour of the entertainment industry.

Editorial Credits:
Editor: Alison Deering
Designer: Heidi Thompson and Kayla Rossow
Media reseacher: Pam Mitsakos
Production specialist: Tori Abraham

Image Credits:
Alamy: Moviestore collection Ltd., 54; Getty Images: Brad Barket, 11 top left, Dan Kitwood, 56, top right, Hero Images, 25 top left, Irfan Khan, 57, Jupiterimages, 26 middle right, Lilly Roadstones, 16 top left, Xavier Arnau, 24 top right; Newscom: FOX SEARCHLIGHT PICTURES/Album, 15, Karl-Josef Hildenbrand/dpa/picture-alliance, 43, 46, Tony Bock/ZUMA Press, 45 middle right; Shutterstock: 9387388673, 6 top right, Aaron Amat, 34 top left, Aaron Lim, 50 bottom right, Africa Studio, 17 bottom, Aila Images, 60 top right, Alex Emanuel Koch, 38, Andrey_Popov, 25 middle right, antb, 21 top left, arek_malang, 49 bottom right, bikeriderlondon, 31 middle right, Darrin Henry, 37 top right, Dean Drobot, 45 top right, DJ Mattaar, 28, Don Mammoser, 7 top right, Gaagen, 44 bottom right, Galushko Sergey Alekseewisch, 22 top right, Gelpi, 37 top left, Golden Pixels LLC, 35 top right, Golubovy, 19 top left, goodluz, 22 bottom right, g-stockstudio, 8, 18, 20, 24 bottom right, 52 bottom right, hangingpixels, 35 top middle, ibreakstock, 26 top right, imging, 34 bottom right, Ivan Cholakov, 59, Ivan_Sabo, 6 top left, Jacob Lund 16 bottom right, javitrapero.com, 4, Jerome Kundrotas, 21 bottom, jgolby, 9 top right, Joe Seer, 12, 13, Karramba Production, 52 top left, KPG Payless, 60 left, Kzenon, 11 bottom, Lilyana Vynogradova, 41 middle right, Linda Moon, 61, LOFTFLOW, 52 middle left, Looker_Studio, 19 top right, MAD_Production, 5, Mark Poprocki, 22 middle right, Mayskyphoto, 40 bottom right, Mazan Xeniya, 1, michaeljung, 30, mikecphoto, 44 middle left, MilanMarkovic78, cover top middle, Milles Studio, 24 middle right, mimagephotography, 37 top middle, Monkey Business Images, 23, Northfoto, 33 top left, Pavel L Photo and Video, 39 top left, 40, middle right, 44 top left, PedkoAnton, 41 top left, PHILIPIMAGE, cover bottom, racorn, 35 top left, 36 middle left, Rawpixel.com, 10 middle right, 29 bottom left, Razvan Ionut Dragomirescu, 55, Riccardo Piccinini, 17 top left, Rido, 10 middle left, Samuel Borges, 36 top left, SpeedKingz, 17 top right, Stephen Coburn, 33 bottom left, Stock image, 36 bottom middle, stocklight, 48, Sue Stokes, 29 middle left, swinner, 42 bottom left, Terence Walsh 31 middle left, VisionDive, 42 bottom middle, Vitalii Nesterchuk, 42 bottom right, Vlad Teodor, 7 top left, wavebreakmedia, 19 top middle, 32, 50 top left, 58, Woraphon Nusen, 42 middle right, Yeko Photo Studio, 6 bottom right; Thinkstock: dolgachov, 49 top left, HASLOO, 53 top right

Design Elements: Shutterstock: Africa Studio, cobalt88, Flas100, igor.stevanovic, Kristina Postnikova, helen-light, optimarc, pan_kung, pashabo

Source Credits: p. 14 from www.newyorker.com/magazine/2009/11/09/talk-this-way; p. 15 from www.newyorker.com/magazine/2009/11/09/talk-this-way and www.inklingsnews.com/b/2010/04/16/tim-monich-the-man-behind-the-voices; p. 41 from www.dailystar.co.uk/real-life/364199/Hollywood-s-top-stunt-artist-is-a-gritty-British-superwoman; p. 50 from www.cinemablend.com/reviews/X-Men-Apocalypse-70137.html; pg. 51 from www.rollingstone.com/movies/reviews/the-jungle-book-20160413, www.rogerebert.com/reviews/alice-through-the-looking-glass-2016, www.cinemablend.com/reviews/Captain-America-Civil-War-69827.html, www.rollingstone.com/movies/reviews/star-wars-the-force-awakens-20151216, and www.rollingstone.com/movies/reviews/the-divergent-series-allegiant-20160318

Printed in Canada.
010039S17

Table of Contents

PROD. NO.
SCENE
TAKE
ROLL
DATE
SOUND
PROD. CO.
DIRECTOR
CAMERAMAN

INTRODUCTION

On the Big Screen

Are you one of the millions of people who flock to movie theaters each week? Maybe you love cheering for your favorite superhero as he or she battles to save the world from destruction. Maybe you race along with the speeding fighter jets as they dive and roll through the atmosphere in 3-D. Or maybe you try to solve the mystery before the hero.

A BEHIND-THE-SCENES LOOK AT A BEACH SHOOT FOR THE MOVIE *RUTA MADRE*

The best movies whisk people away to new worlds and make them feel as if they are part of the action. But what happens on the big screen requires a tremendous amount of action behind the scenes. When most people think about dream jobs in movies, they think about the glamorous actors or directors and producers. But if you've ever watched the scrolling end credits, you know that hundreds of people work on every movie. These behind-the-scene jobs make the actors' characters larger than life for audiences.

If you're reading this, you are likely more than just a fan of films. You want to be a part of the movie business. You want to use your talents and love of movies to build a career in the film industry. And while the entertainment industry is competitive, the good news is, the career possibilities are endless — from using your creative writing ideas as a scriptwriter or film critic to sharing your love of animals as an animal actor trainer. Each job needs savvy people like you who know there's no business like show business.

CHAPTER 1

Talent Agent

When actors are busy performing, they don't always have time to find their next job. That's where talent agents come in. Talent agents make it their business to know everything that's happening in entertainment. They know which actors have been cast in which movies. They keep in daily contact with directors and producers so they know what film projects are up next.

It's often said that the difference between an aspiring actor and a working actor is a good agent. As a talent agent, it's up to you to find your clients roles that will further their careers. That involves reading lots of scripts. You must be familiar with available roles and pending projects in order to pitch clients to studios, directors, producers, and casting directors. Talent agents must also know their clients' strengths and weaknesses. This knowledge helps determine which casting calls to send clients to. If actors have live performances, agents often attend to get to know their clients better. The actors' experiences help agents select auditions.

At a Glance

Also known as: Talent manager
Overview: Talent agents manage the people who make movies, in particular actors.
Education: College degree in the liberal arts or business; acting and film classes
Special skills: Good people and negotiation skills, calm under pressure, organized, persuasive, and detailed
Salary: $28,060–$111,370 (and more) with an average salary of $62,940/year; pay is earned based on percentage of talents' income.

A strong agent is also a strong negotiator. After all, it's up to the agent to use his or her film industry connections to negotiate the best deals for clients. For example, an agent may try to get a client a share of the profits from a film's ticket and DVD sales. If stores will sell toys based on the movies, agents try to get a piece of the profits from those

sales. More money for a client means more money in an agent's pocket; actors pay their agents a percentage of their movie deals.

GET IN THE SCENE

Agents need to be persuasive, confident, and outgoing. Perfect these skills by:

- Joining the debate team
- Reading and writing persuasive essays
- Practicing sales pitches with fundraisers
- Running for student government office (or campaigning for a friend) and convincing others why they should vote for you or your candidate

A large part of an agent's job involves networking. This can be a glamorous perk. Agents attend parties, awards shows, movie premieres, and other events where famous actors, directors, and producers are on the guest list. As an agent, it's important to be outgoing and personable. You must be able to make friends fast, act with confidence, and trust your instincts about both people and the film industry. Agents know they need good relationships with people in the movie business, so it pays to keep in touch. After all, wouldn't you rather work with a trusted friend than a stranger?

Agents sometimes contact famous actors, hoping to represent them for their next starring roles. They also spend time scouting new talent. They attend theater performances to check out potential clients. Up-and-coming actors also send résumés and

performance clips to agents hoping to earn representation. In some states and countries, agents must be licensed to represent actors. Most agents belong to a union such as the Screen Actors' Guild (SAG), which allows them to represent actors who belong to the union.

SAG-AFTRA

More than 160,000 entertainment professionals belong to the Screen Actors' Guild and American Federation of Television and Radio Artists (SAG-AFTRA). This union represents people in the movie industry, such  as actors, voiceover artists, and stunt performers. Singers, recording artists, puppeteers, and dancers also join SAG-AFTRA. This union represents the entertainment professionals and helps them in their careers. Members pay joining fees and yearly dues to stay in the union. In return, the union protects its members' rights to safe working conditions.

To join, performers must prove they are eligible for membership. They can do this in one of three ways:

- Provide proof that they held a job as a leading performer or recording artist. The role must be a major speaking job in a SAG film, video, television show or commercial. (Proof may be a signed contract or a pay stub.)
- Provide proof of a minimum of three days work as an extra or background actor. (This is the most common way a performer qualifies to join.)
- Provide proof that they worked as a lead actor or singer under another performers' union connected to SAG-AFTRA for at least one year.

CHAPTER 2
Dialect Coach

Have you ever noticed how an actor can speak with an impeccable British accent in one film and sound like a native German speaker in another? More than likely they worked with a dialect coach to learn each accent. And if you have a knack for perfecting accents or imitations, this might be the perfect career for you!

As a dialect coach, you will teach an actor how to change his or her speech patterns — and sometimes even body language — to match a character's native language. Dialect coaches work with actors until the actors can speak naturally with the new dialect or accent. When dialect coaches do their job, actors' speech rhythms and body movements make their characters believable and authentic to movie audiences.

While training for a role as Amelia Earhart, actress Hilary Swank used dialect coach Tim Monich. "When you're in the scene and you're thinking about the accent, you don't have it," Swank said. "At some point, though, it just clicks, and I can let go then of where my jaw goes and where my tongue should be."

At a Glance

Also known as: Accent coach

Overview: A dialect coach helps actors speak in certain dialects or accents.

Education: College degree in liberal arts; master's degree in voice studies, speech, phonetics, or language; acting experience

Special skills: An ear for language; being able to hear what makes a language, accent, or dialect unique; ability to teach this to others; excellent communication skills; patience

Salary: $18,000–$70,000/year with an average salary of $33,850/year

FIRST-PERSON PERSPECTIVE: DIALECT COACH TIM MONICH

Tim Monich taught Brad Pitt to speak as if he were from somewhere deep in the mountains of Tennessee. He taught Matt Damon to speak as if he were South African. For Hilary Swank's role as Amelia Earhart in *Amelia,* he helped her speak like someone originally from Kansas but who lived near Philadelphia while attending school.

Monich always starts with language lab exercises that require actors to listen to a word and then repeat it. "I'm listening for something slightly off," he says. "It could be the actual vowel, it could be the placement or emphasis, the vocal quality — too nasal, too throaty, too gravelly. It could be too long."

Monich says one of the best parts of his job is the people. "Almost everyone I've gotten to work with is really fun, nice, and interesting." He admits to getting star struck once in his career when he coached Sophia Loren. "I have enjoyed almost every job that I have had, I have to say. Maybe I'm just easy to please, but the quality of people that I get to work with is pretty extraordinary, so what's not to like?"

HILARY SWANK IN *AMELIA*

Dialect coaches help actors master an accent so well that even locals have trouble determining if an actor is a native speaker. How? First, coaches teach actors how to listen to a dialect to find its patterns. They point out the differences in vowels or consonants compared to the actors' own dialects. Maybe the vowels are longer or shorter. The consonants might be more forceful, softer, or even missing.

GET IN THE SCENE

- Study as many cultures and languages as you can. Note their origins, history, and dialects. How did the languages change over time?
- Keep notes on languages and learn what makes each language sound like it does. You don't need to speak languages fluently to be able to recognize what language it is.
- Watch films and study the actors' accents. Try to imitate the actors' voices.

But it's not just the sounds that are important. Body language plays a part as well. Coaches show videos of native speakers to help actors find the rhythms of speech. They point out how a native speaker's lips, jaws, tongue, teeth, and cheeks move while speaking. Native speakers may drop or tense up their jaws when saying certain words. Their lips may round instead of relax. Maybe their tongues press against their front teeth for certain sounds.

As a dialect coach, you get to give actors homework. You'll tell an actor to practice his or her lines in a mirror in order to see the movement of the mouth. This is helpful since actors' facial muscles may need to learn new movements for new sounds. You might also ask actors to record themselves speaking and then play back the recordings to listen for places to improve.

CHAPTER 3

Screenwriter

What do all movies have in common? Every single one starts with a script. Writers get script ideas from all sorts of inspiration. Some are original stories from the writer's imagination. Others may be based on news stories, history, books, or even religious or mythical stories. A screenwriter writes the script that becomes the road map for a movie. This map contains the dialogue and action that will be spoken and performed by the actors. If you have a gift for envisioning stories in your mind, then scriptwriting might be your ticket to the big screen.

Most scriptwriters work on speculation, which is often shortened to "on spec." This means they write the scripts first and then try to sell them to producers. Whether you've sold previous screenplays or just completed your first one, it's your job as the writer to make a director love it. You'll need to find someone who believes your screenplay will be a success before you see your words come to life on the big screen.

At a Glance

Also known as: Scriptwriter

Overview: A screenwriter writes scripts on which films are based; these works may be original or adaptations from books, news stories, or other sources.

Education: College degree in writing or screenwriting; additional film degree is very helpful

Special skills: Excellent creative writing skills and a thorough knowledge of motion picture production

Salary: $29,000–$114,000/year with an average salary of $60,250/year

Screenwriters often begin with a cast of characters. Knowing your characters' ages, hair colors, and places of birth is just the starting point as a screenwriter. Screenwriters spend time watching people around them

to understand how and why people act, move, and speak. When you give your characters fears, flaws, and goals, you'll create characters that make movie audiences laugh, cry, or clench their fists.

GET IN THE SCENE

- Read — Developing a good screenplay starts with storytelling. What better way to familiarize yourself with stories than to read lots of them?
- Study — Become a good researcher, so that your screenplays are accurate and believable. Also study writing styles — what books make you laugh or cry? Figure out why.
- Write — The more you write, the better you will be at it. Try imitating your favorite writers. Write for the school newspaper, or write a play for friends or classmates to perform.
- Attend film festivals — Often you may get to meet screenwriters who penned the films being shown.
- Watch lots of movies — comedies, romances, adventure, action, etc. Each kind uses different techniques to set the movie's tone. Make note of camera movements, sound effects and music used, and dialogue.

As a screenwriter, you want to *show* the audience what is happening, rather than just *telling* them. You want to create dialogue and action that makes moviegoers sit on the edges of their seats to find out what happens next. Dialogue must be realistic and believable. Writers include body language cues within the script as a way to add depth to characters. For instance, a character might feel nervous about taking a test. Adding body language details such as making the character squeeze her hands together, tap her left foot, or glance repeatedly at her neighbor's test paper *shows* the audience how she's feeling.

Once your screenplay is complete, it's time to send it into the movie production market. If you have written your screenplay on spec, you'll send copies to motion picture studios and producers, along with a short summary of your script's story. If a company wants to make your script into a movie, it will make an offer to buy the screenplay. As the writer, you can then accept, counter, or outright reject the offer.

Once purchased, screenplays become shooting scripts, also called production scripts. In this version of your script, you'll work with the film production crew to add technical instructions, such as film editing notes, camera angles, fade-outs, locations of shots, and props needed for every scene.

FAST FACT

Scripts or screenplays must be written in a specific format. They usually have between 90 and 120 pages, depending on the type of movie. Shorter movies, such as comedies, run around 90 minutes. Dramas run longer — about two hours. How do writers know how long their movie script is? They type their scripts using **Courier 12 point font.** One properly formatted script page equals about one minute of screen time. So, a 140-page screenplay will become a 140-minute movie.

The man in black shoots open a window, climbs on a Dumpster, and jumps dark warehouse.

The officer sprints down the alley with flashlight and gun drawn, and follows him through the warehouse window

INT. WAREHOUSE – NIGHT

               OFFICER
Police! Drop your weapon and put your hands in the air!

             MAN IN BLACK
(Laughing) Do you really think you're going to stop me?

             OFFICER
Don't move, or I'll shoot!

             MAN IN BLACK
If you want me, come and get me.

The man in black disappears behind a tall row of stee cylinders and cranks open a valve on one of them.
pressurized gas HISSES out.

SCRIPT LINGO

Abbreviation	Meaning
EXT	exterior (outside) setting
INT	interior (inside) setting
I/E	interior/exterior
OS	off-screen
DISS	dissolve shot
F/I	fade in

CHAPTER 4

Casting Director

Matching the right actors with leading roles in movies can be the difference between a hit film and a box-office flop. That's why directors, producers, studios, and film production companies hire casting agents. Like talent agents, casting directors keep up-to-date with the acting world. They know which actors starred in certain movies and what roles actors have performed best and worst. An extensive knowledge of movies — along with good instincts — helps casting directors decide who would do well in upcoming roles.

Casting directors rub elbows with movie stars, directors, and producers. To do this well, you'll need to have an outgoing, friendly personality. Those qualities will help you build relationships with people in the film industry.

As a casting agent, it is your job to hire the actors who will appear in a movie. First your director will send you the movie script to read. Then you'll meet to discuss the director's and producer's visions for the leading and supporting cast. Following the meeting, you'll get to work breaking down the script into scenes. You'll take notes on what characters are in each, their traits, and how many lines they speak. Then, you'll combine the director's creative vision of each character with your script notes to write character profiles. Then the search is on to find the perfect cast.

Casting agents need to be choosy. That means studying tons of data to find the right actor for a part. Casting directors spend a large amount of time researching portfolios, websites, and files. They check out hundreds of photos and résumés of possible actors. They search for undiscovered talent by attending theatrical plays, going to comedy clubs, and watching small-budget films.

At a Glance

Also known as: Casting agent

Overview: A casting director decides what roles need to be filled for scripts and finds, auditions, and hires actors for movies.

Education: College degree in film studies or acting or a degree in business and communications

Special skills: Knowledge of SAG–AFTRA rules and how to hold auditions; excellent networking and teamwork skills; organized

Salary: $31,780–$181,780 (and more) with an average salary of $68,440/year

Sometimes a director may provide an actor wish list for a film. As a casting agent, it's up to you to contact each actor's agent to see if an actor is available and interested in reading a script. If the actors want to perform in the movie, you'll negotiate their contracts with their agents.

Casting directors may also hold open casting calls and organize formal auditions. During casting calls, casting agents and directors listen to actors read parts of the script or watch actors perform rehearsed scenes designed to showcase their talents. Once the team selects the best actors, the casting agent gets to break the good news to an actor and his or her agent.

GET IN THE SCENE

Casting directors know how to spot talent.

They also know the film industry and how to build relationships with actors, agents, directors, and producers. Here are some ideas for you to get started:

- Attend film festivals. You may meet actors, directors, and producers of featured films.
- Watch movies and think critically about actors. Would you have cast any characters differently? Why or why not?
- Help cast a school theater production. Volunteer to read the script, summarize the characters needed, write the casting call, and sit in on auditions.
- Get involved with school or local theater productions. Gain experience by acting in or producing shows (set design and construction, light and sound crews, etc.).

AUDITION NOTES FOR *THE GREATEST MOVIE EVER*

AN EXAMPLE OF CASTING DIRECTOR NOTES AFTER AN AUDITION

Girl #1:
- friendly personality
- has experience in college theater
- well-prepared with monologue for the character she was auditioning for
- had trouble with American accent
- showed a passion for the film and character

Girl #2:
- 25 years old — perfect age for character
- fun, outgoing personality
- has a degree in filmmaking
- gave an emotional monologue showing an acting range needed for this film
- very passionate about this film and acting as a career
- came with references from previous directors

Girl #3:
- good audition; well-prepared
- friendly personality, though quiet
- college degree in education
- acts in local theater
- has the look we're seeking

Boy #1:
- university student
- monologue was really short
- forgot his lines and stumbled over words
- has acted as an extra in a few films
- when asked why he wanted this role, he didn't give a concrete answer

Boy #2:
- 19 years old
- outgoing and friendly personality
- acted as lead in several college and local theater productions
- demonstrated singing and dancing ability that ties to the film's character
- didn't come prepared with a monologue, but read well from the script
- accent needs work

Boy #3:
- conceited and aloof personality; may prove difficult to work with on set
- great American accent
- late for audition; claimed traffic was bad
- has the look we're seeking

CHAPTER 5

Location Scout

Have you ever wanted to visit a tropical island you've seen in a movie? Or maybe you've wondered how a movie director found that underwater ocean cave or those lush, green hills surrounding an ancient castle? They probably used a location scout. And if you love to travel and explore the destinations off the beaten path, this just might be the career for you.

Before a location scout heads out to explore the world, he or she must first read through the script and make a list of all settings needed. Then the scout meets with the director and production crew to create a wish list for movie locations. Does the director want a long, winding highway lined with forests? Does one scene call for haunted houses and another take place in a busy airport? With production notes in hand, the location scout then goes out and finds the real places that match the movie settings.

As a location scout, your packing list should always include your camera and notepads. Scouts snap location photos from all angles and at different times of day and night. This helps the art directors and camera operators determine what the lighting is like. They explore the surrounding locations. Are there noisy airports, highways, or industrial factories that will create unwanted noises for the film? Or maybe a residential neighborhood or school is nearby, making the explosion scenes impossible.

Movies have multiple settings, and a location scout has to find them all. Sometimes real-world settings need to be changed to suit the movie. Changes may be large, such as paving or building roads, or small, such as removing a rooftop satellite dish or changing a store sign.

Even if a location doesn't require changes, scouts must get written permission to use the locations. Scouts need to have outgoing, friendly personalities to build good relationships with the people in charge. If a scout can prove to the local people that he or she is trustworthy and responsible, it will make the job easier when crews are setting the scenes and filming the action.

GET IN THE SCENE

- Watch lots of movies and look for stunning settings. Keep an eye out for locations you think are comparable.
- Take landscape photos from different angles and at different times of day.
- Make notes of different locations — what types of films work there?
- Keep a digital photo book of your research.
- Take photography classes or read books and watch videos on photography.
- If you take trips, bring along your camera and notes to start your location files.

Once filming begins, scouts become location managers. In this role you'll be first on set and last to leave. You'll bo the go-to person if problems arise. The location manager rents equipment such as electrical generators. He or she arranges tents or trailers for the makeup and hair teams and orders meals for the actors and crew.

At a Glance

Also known as: Location manager
Overview: A casting director finds the right places to film scenes for a movie, obtains permission to use locations, and manages them once filming begins.
Education: College degree in film or fine arts
Special skills: Efficient at research; persuasive; communicates well; good at photography; team player
Salary: $31,082–$133,376/year with an average salary of $64,363/year

CHAPTER 6
Script Supervisor

Picture this scene: A man in a red shirt is sitting down at a table to eat dinner with his family. The camera cuts away, and you see one of the children slipping two of her five Brussels sprouts into her lap. The camera cuts back to the man — his shirt is now blue. The view switches back to the girl who just got caught hiding her unwanted vegetables. You notice the sprouts on her plate have doubled.

Continuity errors such as these sometimes happen in movies. So whose job is it to keep track of these details? That task falls to the script supervisor. If you're the kind of person who has a keen eye for details, this behind-the-scenes movie career might be for you.

ACTOR RICHARD GERE ON THE SET OF *ARBITRAGE*

GET IN THE SCENE

Script supervisors need to pay attention to the tiniest details. Here are some ideas you can try now to see if this career is for you:

• Carefully watch films, and pay attention to details. Did you find any errors or inconsistencies? Sometimes watching a film frame-by-frame will reveal mistakes.

• Volunteer for school productions or local theater to take detailed scene notes (or just try this on your own) during rehearsals. Make notes on characters' clothing, props, locations of everyone and everything, the lighting, etc.

• Take photos. Cameras are essential for a script supervisor's job.

• Practice your note-taking abilities; you must be clear, yet brief, and well organized.

• Play memory skills games — card-flipping match games and number sequences are good examples

One of the most crucial tools a script supervisor has is a continuity binder. This is where you'll keep track of the details from every scene. A script supervisor also carries a stopwatch to time every take. You'll add these times to your notes. You'll also need a copy of the script. As continuity coordinator, it's your responsibility to cue actors when they forget their lines, so you read along as the scenes unfold.

CONTINUITY BOOK

As a script supervisor, you'll carry a continuity book everywhere on set. This is where you'll write notes about each take for every scene. The book is filled with detailed notes on:

- Actors' wardrobes, actions, lines, hair and makeup, positions and locations in the scene, and props they are holding
- Camera angles and lenses used
- Timing — was the scene shot in slow motion, freeze time, normal, or fast forward?
- Focus changes — when did the cameras zoom in and out?
- Setting details, such as time of day, artwork on the wall, and furniture arrangements

At a Glance

Also known as: Continuity coordinator

Overview: A script supervisor keeps track of the different takes during shooting and takes detailed notes for the director and editor.

Education: High school graduate or college degree in communications or film

Special skills: Detail-oriented — able to observe and record the smallest things; effective communicator; organized

Salary: $25,303–94,623/year with an average salary of $69,235/year

Continuity coordinators also keep a digital camera handy. Photos capture details you may not have time to write down in your binder. You'll snap hundreds of photos to help you recall details when it's time to reset scenes for additional takes. These photos can be crucial to re-creating scenes, since shots of the same scene can be taken days or weeks apart. And most of the time, scenes are shot out of order based on factors such as weather, location availability, or actors' schedules. Sometimes the ending of a movie is filmed months before the beginning!

When filming is finished, the script supervisor isn't done. Now it's time to put on your editing hat to piece together the director's favorite individual takes. Your notes will help organize and combine the takes into a completed film.

SCRIPT SUPERVISORS KNOW EVERYTHING

What might a script supervisor need to know? Check out some examples of questions that might need to be answered behind the scenes:

- Hair stylist: "Was she wearing the red or pink headband?"
- Makeup artist: "Was she crying in this shot?"
- Actor: "Was my shirt buttoned?"
- Dolly grip: "On what word does she cross to the window?"
- Best boy: "What's the cue to raise the lights?"
- Actress: "Do I have my left knee crossed over my right? Or right over left?"
- Prop master: "Was the window open or closed?"
- Special effects: "Is the tea pot steaming?"
- Boom operator: "Where was she when she screams?"

CHAPTER 7
Stunt Performer

Movie characters flip speeding cars, fall from galloping horses, and leap off of high cliffs into swirling river rapids below. They explode through windows or catch fire. How do actors do all of these steal-your-breath stunts that make movies so exciting? Most of the time, they don't. When movie scenes call for dangerous stunts, professional stunt doubles step into the actors' shoes. If you love extreme sports and pushing yourself to the limit, check out what it takes to be a stunt performer.

The best stunts make audiences gasp or hide their eyes because it seems as if there's no way out for the actors. But movie stunts only *appear* out of control. In reality, stunt doubles spend hours planning, designing, rehearsing, and performing every stunt to make sure it's safe. In your training as a stunt double, you'll learn that safety comes first in every stunt.

GET IN THE SCENE

- Play as many sports as you can.
- Take martial arts classes.
- Take care of your body. Eat healthy foods, and get plenty of sleep.
- Stay physically fit through dance, horseback riding, swimming, or other aerobic activities on a regular basis.

At a Glance

Also known as: Stuntman; stuntwoman; stunt double
Overview: A stunt person performs the dangerous physical actions that actors cannot or prefer not to do.
Education: Athletic training; stunt training; safety instruction
Special skills: Excellent physical condition; excels at several sports and extreme sports; daredevil with knowledge of how to stay safe; acting experience helps
Salary: $853/day or $3,200/week (according to SAG) with an average salary of $70,000/year

In stunt school, performers learn how to use safety equipment designed for stunts. For instance, for fire stunts performers wear fire-resistant long underwear or suits, plus gloves and masks. All of it is coated in fire-protectant gel. For car chase or car wreck scenes, drivers are highly trained, and cars are equipped with safety harnesses and roll cages. Whenever any dangerous stunt is performed, medical and fire safety crews stand by to help if something goes wrong.

WHAT DID YOU LEARN IN SCHOOL TODAY?

Most stunt performers attend classes at professional stunt schools. These schools train performers how to:

- Fall, flip, and then land into air bags
- Use air rams that propel them into the air during explosions on set
- Set up and use decelerators that slow their falls from buildings
- Use wires and cables to create the appearance of flight or levitation.
- Use ratchets that yank performers backward through the air with attached cables and then land them safely
- Make movie fights look real by practicing stopping their fists and feet just short of other performers' bodies
- Use trampolines to launch themselves into foam pits and crash mats
- Crash through windows made of safety glass
- Fall down stairs
- Safely perform fire stunts

Before you can ever jump off a skyscraper or fly through the air after an explosion, you'll need to be in top athletic shape. Physical fitness not only reduces your risk of injuries, it also gives you the strength and stamina to perform physically demanding stunts. Stunt doubles prepare for their careers with years of experience in extreme sports, such as high diving, bungee jumping, drag racing, scuba diving, skydiving, or rock climbing. They also learn martial arts, boxing, and gymnastics. Some even earn pilot's licenses, all before ever working on a movie set.

FIRST-PERSON PERSPECTIVE: STUNT WOMAN ZARENE DALLAS

A HORSEBACK STUNT IN ACTION

For as long as Australian-born stunt performer Zarene Dallas can remember, she has wanted to ride horses in movies. Dallas's love of riding led her to stunt work. "Now I get paid to hang off a horse, walk through fire, or climb up the side of a building," she says.

Dallas's skills include car racing, horse riding, kickboxing, and being set on fire. Because of her diverse stunt abilities, she is one of the film industry's most in-demand stuntwomen. She has appeared in movies such as *Skyfall, Fast and Furious 6,* and *Paddington* and has doubled for famous actresses such as Cameron Diaz and Nicole Kidman. "I have been very lucky to have been offered so much work on so many amazing films and shows," she says.

For Dallas, stunt work is a dream career. "My job is so exciting. Every day is completely different. Even if I am just falling down a hole for the day, I still get such an adrenaline rush every time I'm on set performing a stunt. One day I could be riding horses, the next day I could be in a bar fight or racing a motorbike at high speeds. I absolutely love what I do."

STUNT WORK IN THE UNITED KINGDOM

In the United Kingdom, stunt performers and coordinators must meet certain standards set by the Joint Industry Stunt Committee (JISC) before they can work. Stunt performers must prove they are experts in six or more of the following categories. The categories must fall within at least four groups, and one must be from Group A, but no more than two categories should fall within one group. At least one year's experience is required in each qualification.

- Group A: **Fighting**

    Categories: combat, boxing, or a martial art

- Group B: **Falling**

    Categories: trampoline jumping, high diving

- Group C: **Riding and Driving**

    Categories: motorcycles, cars, horseback riding

- Group D: **Agility and Strength**

    Categories: gymnastics, rock climbing

- Group D: **Water**

    Categories: scuba diving, underwater work, swimming

CHAPTER 8

Sound Effects Designer

Foley artists chop vegetables, smash watermelons, squish cooked chicken, and snap celery stalks in half. These artists aren't chefs — they're experts in sound. They use food and other props to imitate or create sounds for movies. If you think playing with food and other household items sounds like fun, then the creative career of sound effects designer may be on your play list.

During filming, the sound crew positions microphones to capture the actors' dialogue. This means the background sounds — noises such as clacking horse hooves, swishing clothing, and clicking locks — are not recorded loudly enough. These noises must be added later. It's up to the sound effects designer to re-create these background noises in a realistic way.

Foley artists, named after sound effects pioneer Jack Foley, work in Foley studios to record sounds. Foley studios come equipped with many different floor surfaces, including carpet, linoleum, concrete, and sand. Sound designers keep keys to jangle, locks to click, and bricks to rub together, just to name a few of their sound effects props.

GET IN THE SCENE

- Listen to movies with your eyes closed. What sounds can you identify? What do the sounds you hear tell you about what's happening onscreen?
- Work for your school's radio or TV station.
- Be part of the sound effects team at your local theater. Learn about microphones, sound mixing equipment, and recording equipment.
- Listen and make note of background noises wherever you go. Watch movies and listen for similar noises in similar settings. Did anything seem to be missing or unusual?

As part of the sound effects team, you'll watch the unedited movie first and note what sounds need to be added and when. Then you create a sound effects cue sheet listing every sound that needs to be re-created for the movie. Using your cue sheet for each scene, you and your team then collect the props you'll use to make the sounds. Then it's time to make some noise! As the movie plays on a screen in front of you, you and your team switch on the microphones set up to capture your sound effects. On cue, you grab your props to create and record the sounds to match the action.

At a Glance

Also known as: Sound effects editor; sound engineer; audio engineer; audio designer; audio artist; sound artist; Foley artist; creative sound designer

Overview: A sound effects designer is responsible for sound production and editing; he or she also creates and mixes sound in studio to add to films.

Education: College degree in film, music, other liberal arts

Special skills: Knowledge of how sounds affect emotions; team player; creative; musical; expert in working sound equipment

Salary: $22,510–$118,530/year with an average salary of $53,330/year

Sometimes, especially for sci-fi and fantasy movies, sound effects designers must create never-before-heard sounds. For instance, you may need to mix different animal noises, such as lions, tigers, elephants, and alligators, to create a realistic dinosaur roar. Unusual sound recipes such as squishing jelly in a plastic bag and shaking a bag of popped microwave popcorn may create imaginary alien body sounds when blended together. Need futuristic flying car engine noises? Try recording and blending different airplane engine noises. As a sound design engineer, you may slow down, speed up, or play sounds in reverse to create new sounds.

FOLEY FOOTSTEPS

One common sound effect needed for most movies is footsteps. Any shoe lover who tours a Foley Studio would instantly feel right at home. Foley artists keep all kinds of footwear on hand. It doesn't matter if you're a boy or a girl. Every Foley artist needs to know how to walk in high heels just as gracefully as the actor on-screen. And when an actor's tap shoes click on the wooden dance floor, you'll be matching the beat of their dancing feet step-for-step.

To re-create actors' footsteps, Foley artists first decide what type of surface the actors are walking on. Then they note how fast the actors are walking and if they move with a limp or other unusual gait. If an actor is running barefoot across marble floors or racing down stairs, a Foley artist records bare feet slapping against similar surfaces. He or she might also record feet stomping louder or softer, slower or faster, as seen on-screen. If the actor's boots crunch along a gravel road, you slip on a pair of boots and walk on the studio's gravel surface in time with the actor.

SURPRISING WAYS TO CREATE ORDINARY SOUNDS

DESIRED SOUND	WHAT ARTISTS USE
Horse hooves	Bang two halves of coconut shells together
Fire crackling	Popping plastic bubble wrap
Punching noises	Hitting a phone book or bag of sand
Arrow flyby	Whip a thin stick
Bones breaking	Snap celery
Bats flying	Open and close the umbrella quickly
Chainmail	Rattling set of keys
Dog shaking itself dry	Shake a wet mop
Elephant flapping ears	Flicking a leather jacket
Heartbeat	Press and release a plastic trash can lid
Rain on gravel	Sprinkle water on plastic bags
Skiing/ski jump	Slide printer paper over sandpaper or rub printer paper in circles on a desk
Spaceship door opening	Slide a piece of paper out of an envelope
Stone doors moving	Rub two rough stones or bricks together in a slow, circular motion
Unsheathing a sword	Slide a metal baking sheet or spatula off a countertop without lifting it
Vomiting	Squeeze a soaked sponge over a floor or toilet
Bird taking off in flight	Flap a pair of leather or rubber gloves
Rain	Sprinkle rice or sand on a cooking tray
Walking in dry leaves	Crunch cereal flakes
Laser	Hit a tight cable with a stick
Boiling water	Blow into a filled glass of water with a straw

CHAPTER 9
Film Critic

Who doesn't love talking about movies and sharing opinions about them? Discussing an actor's performance or the special effects can be one of the best parts of watching a movie. Now imagine those opinions being published online or in a magazine. And imagine getting paid to do it. Does that sound like your dream job? If so, then you may be the next Roger Ebert.

One perk of being a movie critic is being invited to attend movie screenings. In this career, you'll get to see movies before they are shown in theaters around the world. But being a film critic involves more than just watching a movie and sharing your opinion. You must also be a critical and objective thinker in order to evaluate actors' performances and a movie as a whole. You must also have strong writing and communication skills to turn your thoughts into a review for readers.

GET IN THE SCENE

- See as many movies as you can. Watch them multiple times and try to pay attention to the actors' performances, how the cameras move, the pace of the action, and how you felt while watching the movie and afterward.
- Read about movies. Learn about different directors' styles and how movies are made. The more you know about film, the better you can compare and contrast movies.
- Write film reviews for your school paper. Write and submit movie reviews as a freelance writer for a local newspaper or community newsletter, or start a blog.
- Read and watch professional film critics' reviews. What makes a good review? How do they criticize movies? Do you agree with their analysis and recommendations?

As a critic, you'll need to watch a movie several times before writing your review, focusing on different aspects each time. For example, the first time through, you may take note of how you feel during every scene. If you attend an early screening, you might observe the audiences' reactions — did they laugh, jump, or sigh? Did the audience get the joke or feel the sadness the actors tried to create with their actions and words?

"... after **Days Of Future Past,** you'll be left feeling a little underwhelmed by **Apocalypse,** as there's only so many times that you can watch the world being brought to the edge of obliteration. **X-Men: Apocalypse** still works and entertains, but not quite as emphatically as its predecessors, and it's proof that bigger and louder is not all always better."
— Gregory Wakeman, CINEMABLEND

REVIEWS CAN MAKE OR BREAK A FILM

- "Director Jon Favreau conjures up a magical place to get lost in. . . . *The Jungle Book*, a visual marvel that cuts a direct path to the heart. Favreau, the director of films as diverse as *Elf, Iron Man* and *Chef,* has managed to blend what's best in the jungle stories of Rudyard Kipling and the 1967 animated Disney version into something unique and unforgettable. See it in reach-out-and-touch 3-D if you can, and prepare to be wowed." — Peter Travers, *Rolling Stone*

- "*Alice Through the Looking Glass* . . . the design is at once hideous and bland — like a rough draft of a CGI-driven blockbuster that filmmakers would show to studio bosses only to ask for more time and money to create something releasable. There is not a single effect in the movie that stirs the mind, a single composition that stirs the eye, a single line worth remembering." — Matt Zoller Seitz, RogerEbert.com

- "*Captain America: Civil War* . . . is equally thrilling, fun, engaging, emotional, smart, and thought-provoking, and really everything you want from summer entertainment." — Eric Eisenberg, CINEMABLEND

- "*Star Wars: The Force Awakens* . . . It's everything the kid in us goes to the movies for — marvelous adventure that leaves us surprised, scared and euphoric." — Peter Travers, *Rolling Stone*

- "*The Divergent Series: Allegiant* . . . plods along like a franchise on its last legs. Who remembers where we left off last time in *Insurgent*? My point exactly — no one. . . . Director Robert Schwentke and his trio of writers haven't given us a single reason to hang around for the last installment, due out next year and laughably called *Ascendant* — ironic, considering the only place the misbegotten series is going is down, down, down." — Peter Travers, *Rolling Stone*

The next several times watching a movie, use your knowledge of film and film production to take a deeper look into technical elements. Your readers may want to know if the movie's special effects seemed real and believable. You might take a look at the camera techniques the director used. You may also note if camera movements, such as constantly switching point of view, distracted from the action or dialogue.

Now it's time for you to put your thoughts into writing. Moviegoers rely on reviews to make informed decisions about whether they want to spend their money and time watching a movie. A good writer and critic must be able to turn his or her notes into an entertaining, informative review that gives readers an overview of the film without giving anything away.

REVIEWS CAN BE PUBLISHED ONLINE OR IN PRINT MAGAZINES OR NEWSPAPERS

What if you don't like the movie? When a reviewer finds flaws, he or she must share these with audiences. Maybe the actors' performances were flat and boring. Maybe the dialogue and writing could have been better. Or maybe the special effects flopped. As the movie expert, it's your job to write your reviews objectively. An honest, well-written review will help you earn the trust of movie audiences and readers.

At a Glance

Also known as: Movie critic; reviewer

Overview: A movie critic judges movies and makes recommendations about whether or not people should see them.

Education: College degree in journalism, English, broadcasting, theater, or other liberal arts

Special skills: Excellent writing skills; can work under pressure of deadlines; critical thinking and communication skills

Salary: $32,399–$110,600/year with an average salary of $59,861/year

CHAPTER 10
Visual Effects Artist

As you sit in the theater, ready to watch Spider-Man fly across the screen or animated characters come to life, you have one person in particular to thank — the special effects artist. Instead of paints and canvases, special effects artists use computers and science to make art come alive. They are the ones who make it possible for actors to defy gravity or take on an alien race in another world. And if you're creative and love working with computers, then special effects may be the career for you.

Computer-generated imagery (CGI) is the creation of images and visual effects using computers. Special effects artists use CGI to create characters, environments, objects, and spectacular explosion effects. As a special effects artist, you'll use computer programs to create two- and three-dimensional images and models of background scenery and characters. Then, using computer animation, you'll make those images and models come to life.

Filmmakers rely on the work of visual effects artists to help actors do things human bodies can't. For example, an explosion scene might be too dangerous or too expensive to film in real life. That's where visual effects come into play. In the movie *Independence Day,* director Roland Emmerich asked special effects artists to destroy the White House on film. He used special effects artists to blow it up again in both *2012* and *White House Down.* To make these explosions happen, a special effects artist must research how these scenarios would happen in real life and use creative thinking to turn them into computer images.

Special effects artists must also be familiar with green screen work. When a scene is impossible to film in real life, actors are filmed performing in front of blue or green screens in a studio. Then it's up to special effects artists to fill in the background, creating the world the director envisions, using a computer. Computer-generated backgrounds are then merged with the scenes filmed in studio.

At a Glance

Also known as: Visual effects artist, animator, multimedia artist

Overview: A special effects artist creates visual effects for movies using makeup, computer graphics, models, and camera systems.

Education: Bachelor's degree in special effects, fine arts, or animation

Special skills: Creative thinking, team player, good communication skills, works well under time pressure, excellent drawing and sketching skills, computer programming and graphics skills

Salary: $36,930–$113,600/year (or more) with an average salary of $63,970/year

A special effects artist might also work on cleanup duty after the filming is complete. You could use computer-editing software in post-production to erase things that don't belong in the scene, such as cars parked on the street or people peeking though windows. A director might ask you to add animals, trees, or mountains to the background. Or you could use your computer to combine multiple shots filmed on different days or to add actors and props to scenes.

MOTION CAPTURE

Motion capture is one of the most popular CGI techniques used in movies. Motion capture — or mocap — involves copying the way a person moves and turning those motions into realistic computer models. Mocap allows filmmakers to create realistic animated characters who move like real people, including showing emotions through facial expressions.

In the 2004 animated film *Polar Express,* mocap allowed actor Tom Hanks to play six roles, including the train conductor, without having to put on makeup or change costumes for each part. Instead, he wore a tight body suit covered with tiny markers that reflect light. As Hanks moved, digital cameras tracked the light reflected by the markers and recorded the motion data. The cameras sent all of the captured data to a computer. Special effects artists then matched his movements to the animated characters.

MOCAP STUDIO

BEST VISUAL EFFECTS
ACADEMY AWARD WINNERS (2000–2016)

2000   *The Matrix*

2001   *Gladiator*

2002   *The Lord of the Rings: The Fellowship of the Ring*

2003   *The Lord of the Rings: The Two Towers*

2004   *The Lord of the Rings: The Return of the King*

2005   *Spider-Man 2*

2006   *King Kong*

2007   *Pirates of the Caribbean: Dead Man's Chest*

2008   *The Golden Compass*

2009   *The Curious Case of Benjamin Button*

2010   *Avatar*

2011   *Inception*

2012   *Hugo*

2013   *Life of Pi*

2014   *Gravity*

2015   *Interstellar*

2016   *Ex Machina*

GET IN THE SCENE

Think you have what it takes to make it as a special effects artist in the entertainment industry? Here are some things you can do to get a leg up:

- Take computer programming and computer-aided design classes.
- Take drawing classes and other art classes, including film production.
- Watch films and study the special effects. What techniques did the artists use? What effects were convincing or not so believable?

CHAPTER 11

Hollywood's Looking for You

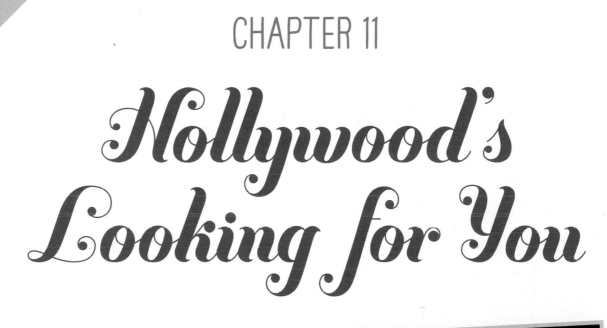

From the initial spark that turns an idea into a screenplay all the way up to a movie's box office release, making a movie takes hundreds of people working together as a team. Film production offers career choices for almost every talent. Creating a box office smash demands clever, hardworking people like you who love the film industry and want to be part of the magic movies create.

And while actors may appear on the big screen, most people in the entertainment industry work behind the scenes to produce thrilling films for audiences around the world. Even though the writers, dialect coaches, agents, and others don't see their names in lights, actors wouldn't be able to wow their fans without talented movie professionals like these behind the scenes. Don't be afraid to start small — work as a personal assistant to someone who has the job you want, or a runner, or someone who does odd jobs around a studio. With passion and hard work, you can work your way into your dream job. One of those behind-the-glamour careers could soon belong to you! Don't keep Hollywood waiting!

READ MORE

Hill, Z. B. *Filmmaking & Documentaries*. Broomall, Pa.: Mason Crest Publishers, 2014.

Mason, Helen. *Makeup Artist*. Creative Careers. New York: Gareth Stevens Publishing, 2014.

Mooney, Carla. *STEM Jobs in Movies*. STEM Jobs You'll Love. Vero Beach, Fla: Rourke Educational Media, 2014.

INTERNET SITES

FactHound offers a fun, safe way to find Internet sites related to this book. All the sites on FactHound have been researched by our staff.

Here's all you do:

Visit www.facthound.com

Type in this code: 9781515748991

ABOUT THE AUTHOR

Danielle S. Hammelef is the author of more than seventeen books for children, including the Capstone Blazer Special Effects series on movies. She has also written award-winning children's magazine stories, nonfiction articles, poetry, and puzzles. Danielle loves to watch animated films and has lost track of how many times she's seen her favorites such as *The Incredibles*, *Shrek*, and *Finding Nemo*. Before becoming a freelance writer, Danielle earned a degree in environmental engineering from Michigan Technological University. Danielle currently lives in Novi, Michigan, with her family.

WANT TO LEARN MORE ABOUT
THE CAREERS BEHIND THE SCENES
IN SOME OF THE WORLD'S MOST
GLAMOROUS INDUSTRIES?

CHECK OUT THESE TITLES TO GO
Behind the Glamour
IN PRO SPORTS, MUSIC, AND FASHION.